The Vocation of the Scholar

By
Johann Gottlieb Fichte

ANODOS BOOKS
Candida Casa

Johann Gottlieb Fichte (1762-1814)
Originally published in 1794, translated by William Smith (1816–1896)
Editing, cover, and internal design by Alisdair MacNoravaich for Anodos Books.
Copyright © 2017 Anodos Books. All rights reserved.

Anodos Books
1c Kings Road
Whithorn
Newton Stewart
Dumfries & Galloway
DG8 8PP

Contents

PREFACE.

THESE LECTURES were delivered last Summer before a considerable number of the young men studying at this University. They form the introduction to a whole which the Author intends to complete, and, when time permits, to lay before the public. A motive—which to mention here would contribute neither to a just estimation of these pages, nor to a right understanding of them—induced him to allow these first five Lectures to be published by themselves. Their being printed just as they were delivered, without the alteration of a single word, must be his excuse for many inaccuracies of expression. In consequence of other occupations, he was unable, even at first, to give to these discourses the polish which he desired. Declamation is a valuable auxiliary in oral communication. To alter them for the press was for a similar reason impossible.

There are in these Lectures many assertions which may not please all classes of readers. But for this the Author is not to blame;—in all his inquiries he has troubled himself very little as to what was likely to please his hearers or be disagreeable to them: Truth alone has been his object,—and what he, according to his best knowledge, held to be true, that he has boldly declared, so far as he was able.

But besides that class of readers who have reasons for their dissatisfaction with what I advance in these Lectures, there are others who hold such speculations as at best *useless*, because they cannot be carried out into practice, and because they find nothing in the actual world, as it is now constituted, at all corresponding thereto;—indeed it is to be feared that the greater number of otherwise honest, respectable, well-behaved, sober-minded people, will thus judge of them. For although, in all ages, those who have been capable of raising themselves to ideas, have always found themselves in a minority,—yet, for reasons which I may well be excused for withholding here, their number has never been less than at the present time. Whilst, within the circle which common experience has drawn around us, men take larger and more general views, and pass more accurate judgments on the phenomena presented to them, than perhaps at any former period; the majority are completely misled and dazzled, so soon as they take a single step beyond this limit. If it be impossible to re-kindle in such minds the once-extinguished sparks of higher genius, we must let them remain without disturbance within that circle; and in so far as they are there useful and necessary, we must not derogate from their value in and for such a sphere. But when they desire to draw down to their own level all

1

to which they cannot raise themselves;—when, for example, they would insist that everything which is printed should be made as practically useful as a cookery-book, or a ready-reckoner, or a service-regulation, and decry everything which cannot so be used,—then indeed do they perpetrate a great wrong.

That the Ideal cannot be manifested in the Actual world, we know as well as they do,—perhaps better. All we maintain is, that the Actual must be judged by the Ideal, and modified in accordance with it by those who feel themselves capable of such a task. Be it granted that they cannot convince themselves of this;—being what they are, they lose very little thereby, and Humanity loses nothing. This alone becomes clear, that they have not been reckoned on in the great plan for the ennoblement of Humanity. This will assuredly proceed on its glorious way;—over them will kindly Nature watch, vouchsafing them, in proper season, rain and sunshine, fitting nourishment and undisturbed digestion, and therewithal comfortable thoughts.

Jena, Michaelmas 1794.

LECTURE I. The Absolute Vocation of Man

THE purpose of the Lectures which I commence to-day is in part known to you. I would answer, or rather I would prompt you to answer for yourselves, the following questions: What is the vocation of the Scholar?—what is his relation to Humanity as a whole, as well as to particular classes of men?—by what means can he most surely fulfil his high vocation?

The Scholar is invested with a special character only in so far as he is distinguished from other men; the idea of his calling arises from comparison, from his relation to Society at large, by which we understand not the State merely, but generally that aggregate of reasonable men who exist near each other in space, and are thus placed in mutual relations with each other.

Hence the vocation of the Scholar, considered as such, is only conceivable in society; and thus the answer to the question, "What is the vocation of the Scholar?" presupposes the answer to another question, "What is the vocation of man in Society?"

Again: the answer to this question presupposes the answer to another still higher; namely this, "What is the absolute vocation of Man?"—i.e. of Man considered simply as man, according to the mere abstract idea of Humanity; isolated and without any relation which is not necessarily included in the idea of himself?

I may be permitted to say to you at present without proof, what is doubtless already known to many among you, and what is obscurely, but not the less strongly, felt by others, that all philosophy, all human thought and teaching, all your studies, especially all that I shall address to you, can tend to nothing else than to the answering of these questions, and particularly of the last and highest of them, What is the absolute vocation of Man? and what are the means by which he may most surely fulfil it?

Philosophy is not essentially necessary to the mere *feeling* of this vocation; but the whole of philosophy, and indeed a fundamental and all-embracing philosophy, is implied in a distinct, clear, and complete *insight* into it. Yet this absolute vocation of Man is the subject of to-day's lecture. You will consequently perceive that what I have to say on this subject on the present occasion cannot be traced down from its first principles unless I were now to treat of all philosophy. But I can appeal to your own inward sense of truth, and establish it thereon. You

3

perceive likewise, that as the question which I shall answer in my public lectures,—What is the vocation of the Scholar? or what is the same thing, as will appear in due time, the vocation of the highest, truest man? is the ultimate object of all philosophical inquiries; so this question, What is the absolute vocation of Man? the answer to which I intend to investigate fundamentally in my private lectures, but only to point out very briefly to-day, is the *primary* object of such investigations. I now proceed to the answer to this question.

What the properly Spiritual in man—the pure Ego, considered absolutely in itself,—isolated and apart from all relation to anything out of itself,—would be?—this question is unanswerable, and strictly taken is self-contradictory. It is not indeed true that the pure Ego is a product of the Non-Ego—(so I denominate everything which is conceived of as existing external to the Ego, distinguished from, and opposed to it:)—it is not true, I say, that the pure Ego is a product of the Non-Ego; such a doctrine would indicate a transcendental materialism which is entirely opposed to reason; but it is certainly true, and will be fully proved in its proper place, that the Ego is not, and can never become, conscious of itself except under its empirical determinations; and that these empirical determinations necessarily imply something external to the Ego. Even the body of man, that which he calls *his* body, is something external to the Ego. Without this relation he would be no longer a man, but something absolutely inconceivable by us, if we can call that *something* which is to us inconceivable. Thus to consider man absolutely and by himself, does not mean, either here or elsewhere in these lectures, to consider him as a pure Ego, without relation to anything external to the Ego; but only to think of him apart from all relation to reasonable beings like himself.

And, so considered,—What is his vocation?—what belongs to him as Man, that does not belong to those known existences which are not men?—in what respects does he differ from all we do *not* call man amongst the beings with which we are acquainted?

Since I must set out from something positive, and as I cannot here proceed from the absolute postulate—the axiom "I am,"—I must lay down, hypothetically in the meantime, a principle which exists indestructibly in the feelings of all men, which is the result of all philosophy, which may be clearly proved, as I will prove it in my private lectures; the principle, that as surely as man is a rational being, he is the end of his own existence; i.e. he does not exist to the end that *something else* may be, but he exists absolutely because *he himself* is to be—his being is its own ultimate object;—or, what is the same thing, man

4

cannot, without contradiction to himself, demand an object of his existence. He is, because he is. This character of absolute being—of existence for his own sake alone,—is his characteristic or vocation, in so far as he is considered solely as a *rational* being.

But there belongs to man not only absolute being, being for itself, but also particular determinations of this being: he not only is, but he is something definite; he does not merely say—"I am," but he adds—"I am this or that." So far as his absolute existence is concerned, he is a reasonable being; in so far as he is something beyond this, What is he? This question we must answer.

That which he is in this respect, he is, not primarily because he himself exists, but because something other than himself exists. The empirical self-consciousness, that is, the consciousness of a determinate vocation, is not possible except on the supposition of a Non-Ego, as we have already said, and in the proper place will prove. This Non-Ego must approach and influence him through his passive capacity, which we call *sense*. Thus in so far as man possesses a determinate existence, he is a *sensuous* being. But still, as we have already said, he is also a reasonable being; and his Reason must not be superseded by Sense, but both must exist in harmony with each other. In this connexion the principle propounded above,—*Man is because he is,*—is changed into the following,—*Whatever Man is, that he should be solely because he is;*—i.e. all that he is should proceed from his pure Ego,—from his own simple personality; he should be all that he is, absolutely because he is an Ego, and whatever he cannot be solely upon that ground, he should absolutely not be. This as yet obscure formula we shall proceed to illustrate.

The pure Ego can only be conceived of negatively, as the opposite of the Non-Ego, the character of which is multiplicity, consequently as perfect and absolute unity; it is thus always one and the same, always identical with itself. Hence the above formula may also be expressed thus; *Man should always be at one with himself,—he should never contradict his own being.* The pure Ego can never stand in opposition to itself, for there is in it no possible diversity, it constantly remains one and the same; but the empirical Ego, determined and determinable by outward things, may contradict itself; and as often as it does so, the contradiction is a sure sign that it is not determined according to the form of the pure Ego, not by itself, but by something external to itself. It should not be so; for man is his own end, he should determine himself, and never allow himself to be determined by anything foreign to himself; he should be what he is, because he wills it, and ought to will it. The

5

determination of the empirical Ego should be such as may endure for ever. I may here, in passing, and for the sake of illustration merely, express the fundamental principle of morality in the following formula: "*So act that thou mayest look upon the dictate of thy will as an eternal law to thyself.*"

The ultimate vocation of every finite, rational being is thus absolute unity, constant identity, perfect harmony with himself. This absolute identity is the form of the pure Ego, and the one true form of it; or rather, by the possibility to conceive of this identity is the expression of that form recognised. Whatever determination can be conceived of as enduring eternally, is in conformity with the pure form of the Ego. Let not this be understood partially or from one side. Not the Will alone should be always at one with itself, this belongs to morality only; but all the powers of man, which are essentially but one power, and only become distinguished in their application to different objects, should all accord in perfect unity and harmony with each other.

The empirical determinations of our Ego depend, however, for the most part, not upon ourselves but upon something external to us. The Will is, indeed, within its own circle—i.e. in the compass of the objects to which it can be applied after they have become known to man perfectly free;—as will be strictly proved at the proper time. But sense, and the conceptions in which it is presupposed, are not free; they depend upon things external to the Ego, the character of which is multiplicity, not identity. If the Ego is to be constantly at one with itself in this respect also, it must strive to operate directly upon the things themselves on which the sensations and perceptions of man depend; man must endeavour to modify these, and to bring them into harmony with the pure form of his Ego, so that his conceptions of them likewise, so far as these (his conceptions) depend upon the nature of their objects, may harmonize with that form. This modification of things according to our necessary ideas of what they *should* be, is not however possible by mere Will, but requires also a certain skill which is acquired and improved by practice.

Further, what is still more important, our empirical determinable Ego receives, from that unrestricted influence of external things upon it to which we subject ourselves without reservation so long as our Reason is still undeveloped, certain tendencies which cannot possibly harmonize with the form of our pure Ego, since they proceed from things external to us. In order to eradicate these tendencies, and restore the pure original form, Will is not sufficient of itself, but we need, besides, that skill which is acquired and improved by practice.

The acquisition of this skill,—partly to subdue and eradicate the improper tendencies which have arisen within us prior to the awakening of Reason and the consciousness of our own independence, —partly to modify external things, and alter them in accordance with our ideas,—the acquisition of this skill, I say, is called Culture; and any particular degree of it, when acquired, is likewise so denominated. Culture differs only in degree, but it is capable of infinite gradations. It is the last and highest *means* to the attainment of the great end of man, when he is considered as of a composite nature, rational and sensuous; complete harmony with himself: it is in itself his ultimate *end* when he is considered only as a sensuous being. Sense should be cultivated: that is the highest and ultimate purpose which can be entertained with respect to it.

The final result of all we have said is as follows: The perfect harmony of man with himself, and that this may be practicable, the harmony of all external things with his necessary practical ideas of them, the ideas which determine what these things *should be;* this is the ultimate and highest purpose of human existence. This harmony is, to use the language of the critical philosophy, the Highest Good; which Highest Good, *considered absolutely*, as follows from what we have already said, has no parts, but is perfectly simple and indivisible, it is the complete harmony of a rational being with himself. But in reference to a rational being who is dependent on external things, it may be considered two-fold; as the harmony of the Will with the idea of an Eternal Will, or, *moral goodness;* and as the harmony of external things with our Will (our rational will, of course), or *happiness.* It is thus, let it be remembered in passing, so far from being true that man is determined to moral goodness by the desire for happiness, that the idea of happiness itself and the desire for it, rather arise in the first place out of the moral nature of man. Not, *That which produces happiness is good;*— but, *That only which is good produces happiness.* Without morality happiness is impossible. Agreeable sensations may indeed exist without it, or even in opposition to it, and in the proper place we shall see why this is the case; but these are not happiness: frequently they are much opposed to it.

To subject all irrational nature to himself, to rule over it unreservedly and according to his own laws, is the *ultimate end* of man; which ultimate end is perfectly unattainable, and must continue to be so, unless he were to cease to be man, and become God. It is a part of the idea of man that his ultimate end must be unattainable; the way to it endless. Hence it is not the *vocation* of man to attain this end. But he may and should constantly approach nearer to it; and thus *the unceasing approximation to this end* is his true *vocation* as man; i.e. as a rational but finite, as a sensuous but free being. If, as we are surely entitled to do, we call this complete harmony with one's self *perfection*, in the highest meaning of the word; then *perfection* is the highest unattainable *end* of man, whilst *eternal perfecting* is his *vocation*. He exists, that he may become ever morally better himself, and make all around him physically, and, if he be considered as a member of society, morally better also, and thus augment his own happiness without limit.

This is the vocation of man considered as isolated, i.e. apart from all relation to reasonable beings like himself. We however are not thus isolated, and although I cannot now direct your attention to the general inter-union of all rational beings with each other, yet must I cast a glance upon the relation with you, into which I enter to-day. It is this noble vocation which I have now briefly pointed out, that I would elevate into perfect clearness in the minds of many aspiring young men —that I desire to make the preëminent object, and constant guide of your lives; young men who are destined on their part again to operate most powerfully on humanity, in narrower or wider circles, by teaching or action, or both, to extend one day to others the culture they have themselves received, and everywhere to raise our common brotherhood to a higher stage of culture; young men, in teaching whom I in all probability teach yet unborn millions of our race. If some among you have kindly believed that I feel the dignity of this my peculiar vocation, that in all my thought and teaching I shall make it my highest aim to contribute to the culture and elevation of humanity in you, and in all with whom you may ever have a common point of contact, that I hold all philosophy and all knowledge which does not tend towards this object, as vain and worthless; if you have so thought of me, I may perhaps venture to say that you have judged rightly of my desire. How far my ability may correspond to this wish, rests not altogether on me; —it depends in part upon circumstances which are beyond our control. It depends in part also on you;—on your attention, which I solicit; on your private diligence, on which I reckon with trustful assurance; on your confidence, to which I commend myself, and which I shall strive to justify by deeds.

LECTURE II. The Vocation of Man in Society

THERE are many questions which philosophy must answer before she can assume the character of knowledge and science: questions which are shunned by the dogmatist, and which the sceptic only ventures to point out at the risk of being charged with irrationality or wickedness, or both.

If I would not treat in a shallow and superficial manner a subject respecting which I believe that I possess some fundamental knowledge, —if I would not conceal, and pass over in silence, difficulties which I see right well,—it will be my fate in these public Lectures to touch upon many of those hitherto almost undisturbed questions without, however, being able to exhaust them completely; and, at the risk of being misunderstood or misinterpreted, to give mere hints towards more extended thought, mere directions towards more perfect knowledge, where I would rather have probed the subject to the bottom. If I supposed that there were among you many of those popular philosophers, who easily solve all difficulties without labour or reflection, by the aid of what they call sound Common Sense, I would not often occupy this chair without anxiety.

Among these questions may be classed the two following, which must be answered, with others, before any natural right is so much as possible;—*first*, By what authority does man call a particular portion of the physical world *his body?* how does he come to consider this body as belonging to his Ego, whereas it is altogether opposed to it?—and *second*, On what grounds does man assume and admit the existence around him of rational beings like himself, whereas such beings are by no means directly revealed to him in his own consciousness?

I have to-day to establish the Vocation of Man in Society; and the accomplishment of this task presupposes the solution of the latter question. By Society I mean the relation of reasonable beings to each other. The idea of Society is not possible without the supposition that rational beings do really exist around us, and without some characteristic marks whereby we may distinguish them from all other beings that are not rational, and consequently do not belong to Society. How do we arrive at this supposition? what are these distinctive marks? This is the question which I must answer in the first place.

"We have acquired both from experience: we know from experience that rational beings like ourselves exist around us, and also the marks by which they are distinguishable from irrational creatures." This might be the answer of those who are unaccustomed to strict philosophical inquiry. But such an answer would be superficial and unsatisfactory; it would indeed be no answer to *our* question, but to an entirely different one. The experience which is here appealed to is also felt by the Egoists, who nevertheless are not thoroughly refuted by it. Experience only teaches us that *the conception* of reasonable beings around us is a part of our empirical consciousness; and about that there is no dispute, no Egoist has ever denied it. The question is, whether there is anything beyond this conception which corresponds to the conception itself; whether reasonable beings exist around us independently of our conceptions of them, and even if we had no such conceptions; and on this matter experience has nothing whatever to teach us so surely as it is only experience; that is to say, the body of our own conceptions.

Experience can at most teach us that there are phenomena which appear to be the results of rational causes; but it can never teach us that these causes actually exist as rational beings in themselves, for being in itself is no object of experience.

We ourselves first introduce such a being into experience; it is only we ourselves who explain our own experience by assuming the existence of rational beings around us. But by what right do we furnish this explanation? This right must be strictly proved before it is made use of, for its validity can only be grounded on its evidence, and not upon its actual use: and thus we have not advanced a single step, but return again to the question with which we set out: How do we come to assume and admit the existence of rational beings around us?

The theoretical domain of philosophy is unquestionably exhausted by the fundamental researches of the Critical School: all questions which still remain unanswered, must be answered upon practical principles. We must try whether the proposed question can be answered on such principles.

The highest impulse in man is, according to our last lecture, the impulse towards Identity, towards perfect harmony with himself; and, in order that he may be in constant harmony with himself, towards the harmony of all external things with his necessary ideas of them. There must not merely be *nothing contradictory* to his ideas, so that the existence or non-existence of an external representative of these ideas might be a matter of indifference to him, but there must actually be *something corresponding* to his ideas. Every idea which exists in the Ego must have a representative, an antitype, in the Non-Ego:—so is his impulse determined.

10

There is in man the idea not only of Reason, but also of reasonable acts and thoughts, and his nature demands the realization of this idea not only within himself but also without himself. It is thus one of his wants that there should be around him reasonable beings like himself.

He cannot create such beings; but he lays the idea of them at the foundation of his observation of the Non-Ego, and expects to find something there corresponding to it. The first mark of rationality which presents itself is of a merely negative character, efficiency founded on ideas, activity towards an end. Whatever bears the marks of design may have a reasonable author; that to which the notion of design cannot be applied has certainly no reasonable author. But this characteristic is ambiguous; the agreement of many things in one end is the mark of design, but there are many kinds of agreement which may be explained by mere natural laws, if not by mechanical, then by organic laws; hence we still require a distinctive mark whereby we may confidently infer from a particular phenomenon the existence of a reasonable cause. Nature proceeds, even in the fulfilment of her designs, *by necessary laws;* —Reason always proceeds *with freedom*. Hence the agreement of many things in one end, *freely fulfilled*, is the sure and infallible characteristic of rationality as manifested in its results. We now inquire, How can we distinguish a phenomenon in our experience produced by necessity, from a phenomenon produced by freedom?

I can by no means be immediately conscious of a freedom which exists out of myself, I cannot even be conscious of a freedom which exists within myself, that is, of my own freedom; for essential freedom is the first condition of consciousness, and hence cannot lie within its sphere of observation. But I may be conscious of this, that I am not conscious of any other cause for a particular determination of my empirical Ego through my will, than this will itself; and this non-consciousness of constraining cause may be called a consciousness of freedom, if this be clearly understood beforehand; and we shall call it so here. In this sense then, man may be conscious of his own free activity.

If through our own free activity, of which we are conscious in the sense above indicated, the character of the activity apparent in the phenomena which experience presents to us is so changed that this activity is no longer to be explained according to the law by which we formerly judged it, but according to that on which we have based our own free action, and which is quite opposed to the former; then we cannot explain this altered view of the activity apparent in experience otherwise than by the supposition that the cause to which we refer it is likewise reasonable and free. Hence arises,—to use the Kantian

11

terminology,—*a free reciprocal activity founded on ideas,—a community pervaded by design;*—and it is this which I call Society. The idea of Society is thus sufficiently defined.

It is one of the fundamental impulses of man to feel that he must assume the existence around him of reasonable beings like himself; and he can only assume their existence under the condition of entering into Society with them, according to the meaning of that word as above explained. The social impulse thus belongs to the fundamental impulses of man. It is man's vocation to live in Society—he *must* live in Society; —he is no complete man, but contradicts his own being, if he live in a state of isolation.

You see how important it is not to confound the abstract idea of Society with that particular empirically-conditioned form of Society which we call the State. Political Society is not a part of the absolute purpose of human life (whatever a great man may have said to the contrary); but it is, under certain conditions, a possible means towards the formation of a perfect Society. Like all human institutions, which are merely means to an end, the State constantly tends towards its own extinction; the ultimate aim of all government is to make government superfluous. Of a surety that time is not now present with us,—and I know not how many myriads, or perhaps myriads of myriads, of years may elapse before it arrive,—(and it must be understood that we have not now to deal with a practical condition of life, but with the vindication of a speculative principle); that time is not now, but it is certain that in the *a priori* fore-ordered course of the human race such a period does exist when all political combinations shall have become unnecessary. That is the time when, in place of strength or cunning, Reason alone shall be acknowledged as the supreme judge of all; acknowledged I say; for although men may even then go astray, and by their errors do hurt to their fellow-men, yet they will then be open to conviction of their error, and, when convinced of it, will be willing to turn back and make amends for their fault. Until that time shall come, mankind, as a race, cannot be true men.

According to what we have said, *free reciprocal activity* is the positive character of Society. It is an end to itself; and hence it exists solely and absolutely for its own sake. This assertion, that Society is its own end, is however not at all incompatible with another, that the form of this association should have a special law which shall give it a more definite aim.

The fundamental impulse of humanity was to discover reasonable beings like ourselves,—or *men*. The conception of man is an ideal conception, because the perfection of man, in so far as he is such, is unattainable. Each individual has his own particular ideal of man in general; these ideals are different in degree, though not in kind; each tries by his own ideal every being whom he recognises as a man. By this fundamental impulse each is prompted to seek in others a likeness to his own ideal; he inquires, he observes on all sides, and when he finds men below this ideal, he strives to elevate them to it. In this struggle of mind with mind, he always triumphs who is the highest and best *man;* and thus from the idea of Society arises that of the *perfection of the race*, and we have thus also discovered the ultimate purpose of all Society as such. Should it appear as if the higher and better man had no influence on the lower and uncultivated, we are partly deceived in our judgment, since we often expect to find the fruit already ripe before the seed has had time to germinate and unfold, and it may partly arise from this, that the better man perhaps stands at too high an elevation above the uncultivated, that they have too few points of contact with each other, and hence cannot sufficiently act upon each other; a position which retards civilization to an incredible extent, and the remedy for which we shall point out at the proper time. But on the whole, the ultimate triumph of the better man is certain: a calming and consoling thought for the friend of humanity and of truth when he looks out upon the open war of light with darkness. The light shall surely triumph at last; we cannot indeed predict the time, but it is already a pledge of victory, of near victory, when darkness is compelled to come forth to an open encounter. She loves concealment, she is already lost when forced out into the open day.

Thus far, then, the result of our inquiries shows, that man is destined for Society; among the capacities which, according to his vocation as laid down in our former lecture, he is destined to improve and perfect, there is also the social capacity.

This destination of man for Society in the abstract, although arising out of the innermost and purest elements of human nature, is yet, as a mere impulse, subordinate to the highest law of constant internal harmony, or the moral law, and by it must be still further defined and brought under a strict rule. When we have discovered this rule, we shall have found *the vocation of man in Society*, which is the object of our present inquiry and of all the considerations we have hitherto set forth.

The social impulse is, in the first place, *negatively* defined by the law of absolute harmony; it must not contradict itself. The impulse leads to *reciprocal* activity, to *mutual* influence, *mutual* giving and receiving, *mutual* suffering and doing, not to mere causality not to mere activity, of which others are but the passive objects. The impulse requires us to discover *free reasonable beings* around us, and to enter into Society with them; it does not demand *subordination* as in the material world, but *co-ordination*. If we do not allow freedom to the reasonable beings whom we seek around us, we take into account merely their theoretical use, not their free practical rationality; we do not enter into Society with them, but we *rule* them as useful animals, and so place our social impulse in opposition to itself. But what do I say? we place our social impulse in opposition to itself? No: rather we do not possess this higher impulse at all; humanity is not yet so far cultivated within us; we ourselves still stand on the lowest grade of imperfect humanity, or slavery. We ourselves have not yet attained to a consciousness of our freedom and self-activity, for then we should necessarily desire to see around us similar, that is, free beings. We are slaves ourselves; and look around us but for slaves. Rousseau says "A man often considers himself the lord of others, who is yet more a slave than they." He might with still greater justice have said "He who considers himself the lord of others is himself a slave." Even should he not bear the outward badge of servitude, yet he has most surely the soul of a slave, and will basely cringe before the first stronger man who subdues him. He only is *free*, who would make all around him free likewise; and does really make them free, by a certain influence the sources of which are hitherto undiscovered. In his presence we breathe more freely; we feel that nothing has power to oppress, hinder, or confine us; we feel an unwonted desire to be and to do all things which self-respect does not forbid.

Man may use irrational things as means for the accomplishment of his purposes, but not rational beings; he may not even use these as means for attaining the end of their own being; he may not act upon them as upon dead matter or upon the beasts, so as to prosecute his designs with them without taking their freedom into account; he may not make any reasonable being either virtuous, or wise, or happy, against his own will. Laying aside the fact that such an attempt would be utterly fruitless, that no being *can* become virtuous, or .wise, or happy, but by his own labour and effort; laying aside the fact that man cannot do this, yet even if he could, or believed he could, he must not even desire to do it; for it is unjust, and by so doing he would be placed in opposition to himself.

The social impulse is also *positively* defined by the law of perfect internal harmony, and thus we arrive at the peculiar vocation of man in Society. All the individuals who compose the human race differ from each other; there is only one thing in which they entirely agree; that is, their ultimate end—perfection. Perfection has but one form; it is equal to itself: could all men become perfect, could they attain their highest and ultimate end, they would all be equal to each other, they would be only one, one single subject. But in Society each strives to make others perfect, at least according to his own standard of perfection; to raise them to the ideal of humanity which he has formed. Thus, the last, highest end of Society is perfect unity and unanimity of all its possible members. But since the attainment of this end supposes the attainment of the destination of each individual man, the attainment of absolute perfection; so it is quite as impossible as the latter, it is unattainable, unless man were to lay aside his humanity and become God. Perfect unity with all the individuals of his race is thus indeed the *ultimate end*, but not the *vocation*, of man in Society.

But to approach nearer this end, constantly to approach nearer it, this he can and ought to do. This approximation towards perfect unity and unanimity with all men may be called *co-operation*. Thus *co-operation*, growing ever firmer at its centre and ever wider in its circumference, is the true vocation of man in Society: but such a *co-operation* is only possible by means of progressive improvement, for it is only in relation to their ultimate destination that men are one, or can become one. We may therefore say that *mutual improvement*,—improvement of ourselves by the freely admitted action of others upon us, and improvement of others by our reaction upon them as upon free beings,—is our vocation in Society.

And in order to fulfil this vocation, and fulfil it always more and more thoroughly, we need a qualification which can only be acquired and improved by culture; and indeed a qualification of a double nature: an ability to *give*, or to act upon others as upon free beings; and an openness to *receive*, or to derive the greatest advantage from the action of others upon us. Of both we shall speak particularly in the proper place. We must . especially strive to acquire the latter, when we possess the former in a high degree; otherwise we cease to advance, and consequently retrograde. Seldom is any man so perfect that he may not be much improved through the agency of *any* other man, in some perhaps apparently unimportant or neglected point of culture.

I know few more sublime conceptions, than the idea of this universal inter-action of the whole human race on itself; this ceaseless life and activity; this eager emulation to give and to receive,' the noblest strife in which man can take a part; this general indentation of countless wheels into each other, whose common motive-power is freedom; and the beautiful harmony which is the result of all. "Whoever thou art," may each of us say "whoever thou art, if thou bear the form of man, thou too art a member of this great commonwealth; through what countless media soever our mutual influence may be transmitted, still by that title I act upon thee, and thou on me; no one who bears the stamp of Reason on his front, however rudely impressed, exists in vain for me. But I know thee not, thou knowest not me! Oh! so surely as we have a common calling to be good, ever to become better,—so surely—though millions of ages may first pass away—(what is time!)—so surely shall a period at last arrive when I may receive thee, too, into my sphere of action, when I may do good to thee, and receive good from thee in return; when my heart may be united to thine also, by the fairest possible bond, a free and generous interchange of mutual influence for good.

LECTURE III. On the Distinction of Classes in Society

The vocation of man as an individual, as well as the vocation of man in society, is now before you. The Scholar is only invested with his distinctive character when considered as a member of society. We may therefore proceed to the inquiry, What is the peculiar vocation of the Scholar in society? But the Scholar is not merely a member of society; he is also a member of a particular class in society: at least it is customary to speak of the Scholar-class—with what propriety or impropriety will appear in due time.

Our chief inquiry—What is the vocation of the Scholar?—thus pre-supposes the solution of a third and very important question, besides those two which we have already answered; this, namely, Whence arises the difference of Classes in Society? or, What is the source of the inequality existing among men?

It will be readily understood without preliminary explanation, that this word *Class* does not mean anything which has come to pass fortuitously and without our aid, but something determined and arranged by free choice for an understood purpose. For an inequality which occurs fortuitously and without our aid, i.e. for physical inequality, Nature is accountable; but inequality of classes seems to be a moral inequality, with respect to which, therefore, the question naturally arises, By what *right* do different classes exist?

Attempts have often been made to answer this question; and enquirers, proceeding merely on the grounds of experience, have eagerly laid hold of and rhapsodically enumerated the numerous purposes which are accomplished by such a division and the many advantages which are gained by it; but by such means any other question may sooner be answered than the one we have proposed. The *advantage* of a certain disposition of things does not prove its *justice;* and we did not propose the historical question, What purpose had man in this arrangement? but the moral question, Whether it was lawful for him to bring it about, whatever purpose he might have had in view by so doing. The question must be answered on the principles of Reason, pure as well as practical; and such an answer has, so far as I know, never yet been even attempted. To prepare for it, I must law down a few general scientific principles.

All the laws of Reason are founded in our spiritual nature; but it is only through an actual experience to which they are applicable that they attain empirical consciousness; and the more frequent such application the more intimately do they become interwoven with this consciousness. It is thus with all the laws of Reason; it is thus especially with the practical, which do not, like the theoretical, terminate in a mere act of judgment, but proceed to an activity without us, and announce themselves to consciousness under the form of *impulses*. The foundation of all impulses lies in our own being: but not more than the foundation. Every impulse must be *awakened* by experience if it is to arrive at consciousness, and must be *developed* by numerous experiences of the same kind if it is to become a *desire*, and its appropriate gratification a *want*, of man. Experience, however, does not depend upon ourselves, and therefore neither does the awakening nor the development of our impulses.

The independent Non-Ego as the foundation of experience or *Nature*, is manifold; no one part of it is perfectly the same as another; this principle is maintained and even strictly proved in the Kantian philosophy. It follows from this, that its action on the human mind is of a very varied character, and nowhere calls forth the capacities and talents of men in the same manner. By these different ways in which Nature acts upon man, are individuals, and what we call their peculiar, empirical, individual character, determined; and in this respect we may say that no individual is perfectly like another in his awakened and developed capacities. Hence arises a physical inequality to which we not only have not contributed, but which we even cannot remove by our freedom; for before we can, through freedom, resist the influence of Nature upon us, we must first have arrived at the consciousness and use of this freedom; and we cannot arrive thereat except by that awakening and unfolding of of our impulses which does not depend upon ourselves.

But the highest law of man and of all reasonable beings, the law of perfect internal harmony, of absolute identity, in so far as this law becomes positive and material by means of special individual applications, demands that all the faculties of the individual shall be uniformly developed, all his capacities cultivated to the highest possible perfection; a demand, the object -of which cannot be realized by the mere law itself; because the fulfilment of the law, as we have said, does not depend upon the law itself, nor upon our will which is determinable by the law, but upon the free action of Nature.

If we apply this law to society, if we assume the existence of reasonable beings around us, then the demand that all the faculties of the individual should be uniformly cultivated includes also the demand that all reasonable beings should be cultivated uniformly with each other. If the faculties of all are essentially the same, as they are, since they are all founded upon pure Reason, if they are all to be cultivated after a similar fashion, which is what the law requires, then the result of such a cultivation must be similar capacities in every respect equal to each other:—and thus by another way we arrive at the ultimate end of all society, as declared in our former lecture,—*the perfect equality of all its members.*

We have already shown in our last lecture that the mere law cannot, of itself, realize the object of this demand, any more than it can realize that of the demand on which our present lecture is founded. But Free-Will can and ought to strive constantly to approach nearer this ultimate end.

And here the activity of the social impulse comes into play, which also proceeds upon this same purpose, and is the means of the requisite continual approximation to its attainment. The social impulse, or the impulse towards mutual cooperation with free reasonable beings as such, includes the two following impulses: *the communicative impulse,* —that is, the impulse to impart to others that form of culture which we ourselves possess most completely, to make others, as far as possible, like ourselves, like the better self within us; and *the receptive impulse,* that is, the impulse to receive from others that form of culture which they possess most completely, and in which we are deficient. Thus defects of Nature in us are remedied by Reason and Freedom; the partial culture which Nature has given to the individual becomes the property of the whole race, and the race in turn bestows all its culture upon him; it gives him all the culture which is possible under the determining conditions of Nature, if we suppose that all the individuals who are possible under these conditions do actually exist. Nature cultivates each individual only in part; but she bestows culture at every point where she encounters reasonable beings. Reason unites these points, presents to Nature a firmly compacted and extended front, and compels her to cultivate *the Race* at least in all its particular capacities, since she will not bestow that culture upon *the Individual.* Reason has already, by means of the social impulse, provided for the equal distribution of the culture thus acquired among the individual members of society, and will provide for it still further; for the sway of Nature does not extend here.

Reason will take care that each individual receive indirectly from the hands of society, the whole and complete cultivation which he cannot obtain directly from Nature. Society will gather together the special gifts of every individual member into a common fund for the free use of all, and thus multiply them by the number of those who share their advantages; the deficiencies of each individual will be borne by the community, and will thus be reduced to an infinitely small quantity: or, to express this in another form more generally applicable, the aim of all culture of human capacity is to subject Nature (as I have defined this expression) to Reason; to bring Experience, in so far as it is not dependent on the laws of our perceptive faculties, into harmony with our necessary practical ideas of Reason. Thus Reason stands in continual strife with Nature. This warfare can never come to an end, unless we were to become gods; but the influence of Nature can and ought to be gradually weakened, the dominion of Reason constantly made more powerful; so that the latter shall gain victory after victory over the former. An individual may perhaps struggle successfully against Nature at his own particular point of contact with her, while at all other points he may be completely subject to her sway. But now society is combined like one man: what the individual could not accomplish by himself, all are enabled to perform by the combined powers of the community. Each indeed strives singly, but the enfeeblement of Nature which is the result of the common struggle, and the partial triumph which each gains over her in his own department, come to the aid of all. Thus even from the physical inequality of individuals arises a new security for the bond which unites them all in one body; the pressure of individual wants, and the still sweeter impulse to supply the wants of others, bind them more closely together; and Nature has strengthened the power of Reason, even while she attempted to weaken it.

Thus far everything proceeds in its natural order: we have found different personalities, various in the kind and degree of their cultivation; but we have as yet no different *classes*, for we have not yet pointed out any special determination of the social impulse by free activity, any voluntary selection of a particular kind of culture. I say, we have not yet been able to show any special determination by means of free activity; but let not this be erroneously or partially understood. The social impulse, considered generally, addresses itself to freedom only; it merely instigates, it does not compel. We may oppose, and even subdue it; we may, through misanthropic selfishness, separate ourselves from our. fellow-men, and refuse to receive anything at the hands of society, that we may not have to render back anything in return; we may, from rude animalism, forget the freedom of society, and look upon it only as something subject to our will, because we have no higher idea of ourselves than as subjects of the power of Nature. But this is not the question here. On the supposition that man obeys the social impulse generally, it is necessary that under its guidance he should impart the advantages which he possesses to those who have need of them, and receive those of which he himself stands in need from those who possess them. And for this purpose there is no need of any particular determination or modification of the social impulse by a new act of freedom, which is all that I meant to affirm.

The characteristic distinction is this: *Under the conditions now laid down*, I as an individual give myself up to Nature for the one-sided cultivation of some particular capacity, because *I must do so;* I have no choice in the matter, but blindly follow her leading. I take all that she gives me, but I cannot take that which she does not give; I neglect no opportunity offered to me of cultivating myself on all sides as far as I can, but I do not create such opportunity, because I cannot create it. If, *on the contrary, I choose a class,*—a class being understood to be something chosen by free will, according to the common use of language, if I choose a class, I must first have become subject to Nature before it was possible for me to choose; for to that end different impulses must be awakened within me, different capacities elevated into consciousness; but *in the choice itself* I determine henceforward to leave entirely out of consideration certain possible opportunities which Nature may perchance offer to me, in order that I may apply *all* my powers and all the gifts of Nature to the exclusive development of *one or more particular capacities;* and by the particular capacity to the cultivation of which I thus devote myself by free choice, will my *class* or *condition* in society be determined.

The question arises, Ought I to choose a particular class? or, if the demand be not imperative, Dare I devote myself to a particular class, that is, to a one-sided culture? If *I ought*, if it be absolute duty, then it must be possible to educe from the highest laws of Reason an impulse directed towards the selection of a class, as we may educe from these laws the impulse towards society in general. If I only *may* do this, then it will not be possible to educe such an *impulse* from the laws of Reason, but only a *permission;* and for the determination of the will to the actual choice thus permitted by Reason, it must be possible to assign some empirical data by means of which, not a law, but only a rule of prudence, may be laid down. How this matter stands will be seen upon further inquiry.

The law says, "Cultivate all thy faculties completely and uniformly, so far as thou canst;" but it does not determine whether I shall exercise them directly upon Nature, or indirectly through intercourse with my fellowmen. On this point the choice is thus left entirely to my own prudence. The law says, "Subdue Nature to thy purposes;" but it does not say that if I should find Nature already sufficiently adapted to certain of my purposes by other men, I should nevertheless myself adapt it to all the possible purposes of humanity. Hence the law does not forbid me to choose a particular class; but neither does it enjoin me to do so, for precisely the same reason which prevents the prohibition. I am now in the field of Free Will; *I may* choose a class, and I must now look out for quite other grounds of determination than those which are derived immediately from the law itself, on which to resolve the question, not "What class shall I choose?"—(of this we shall speak at another time)—but, "Shall I choose any class at all, or shall I not?"

As things are at present, man is born in society. He finds Nature no longer rude, but already prepared in many respects for his purposes. He finds a multitude of men employed in its different departments, cultivating it on every side for the use of rational beings. He finds much already done which otherwise he would have had to do for himself. He might perhaps enjoy a very pleasant existence without ever applying his own powers immediately to Nature; he might even attain a kind of perfection by the enjoyment of what society has already accomplished, and in particular of what it has done for its own cultivation. But this may not be; he must at least endeavour to repay his debt to society; he must take his place among men; he must at least strive to forward in some respect the perfection of the race which has done so much for him.

And to that end two ways present themselves: *either* he may determine to cultivate Nature on all sides; and, in this case, he would perhaps require to apply his whole life, or many lives if he had them, even to acquire a knowledge of what has been already done by others before him and of what remains to do; and thus his life would be lost to the human race, not indeed from evil intent, but from lack of wisdom: *or* he may take up some particular department of Nature, with the previous history of which he is perhaps best acquainted, and for the cultivation of which he is best adapted by natural capacity and social training, and devote himself exclusively to that. In the latter case, he leaves his own culture in its other departments to Society, whose culture in that department which he has chosen for himself is the sole object of his resolves, his labours, his desires; and thus he has selected a class, and his doing so is perfectly legitimate. But still this act of freedom is, like all others, subject to the universal moral law, in so far as that law is the rule of our actions; or to the categorical imperative, which I may thus express: "Never let the determinations of thy will be at variance with thyself;" a law which, as expressed in this formula, may be fulfilled by every one, since the determinations of our will do not depend upon

22

Nature but on ourselves alone.

The choice of a class is a free choice; therefore no man whatever ought to be compelled to any particular class, nor be shut out from any. Every individual action, as well as every general arrangement, which proceeds on such compulsion, is unjust. It is *unwise* to force a man into one class, or to exclude him from another; because no man can have a perfect knowledge of the peculiar capacities of another, and because a member is often lost to society altogether, in consequence of being thrust into an improper place. But laying this out of view, such a course is *unjust* in itself, for it sets our deed itself in opposition to our practical conception of it. We wish to give society a *member*, and we make a *tool;* we wish to have a free *fellow-workman* in the great business of life, and we create an enslaved and passive *instrument;* we destroy the man within him, so far as we can do so by our arrangements, and are guilty of an injury both to him and to society.

We make choice of a particular class, we select one particular talent for more extended cultivation,—*only that we may thereby be enabled to render back to society what it has done for us;*—and thus each of us is bound to make use of our culture for the advantage of society. No one has a right to labour only for his own enjoyment, to shut himself up from his fellow-men, and make his culture useless to them; for it is only by the labour of society that he has been placed in a position wherein he could acquire that culture: it is in a certain sense a product, a property of society; and he robs society of a property which belongs to it if he does not apply his culture to its use. It is the duty of every one, not only to endeavour to make himself useful to society generally, but also to direct all his efforts, according to the best knowledge he possesses, towards the ultimate object of society, towards the ever-increasing ennoblement of the human race; that is, to set it more and more at liberty from the bondage of Nature, constantly to increase its independence and spontaneous activity;—and thus, from the new inequality of classes a new equality arises—a uniform progress of culture in all individual men.

I do not say that human life is at any time such as I have now depicted it; but it *ought to be* so, according to our practical ideas of society and of the different classes it contains; and we may and ought to labour that it may *become* so in reality. How powerfully the Scholar in particular may contribute to this end, and how many means for its accomplishment lie at his disposal, we shall see at the proper time.

When we contemplate the idea now unfolded, even without reference to ourselves, we see around us a community in which no one can labour for himself without at the same time labouring for his fellow-men, or can labour for others without also labouring for himself; where the success of one member is the success of all, and the loss of one a loss to all: a picture which, by the harmony it reveals in the manifold diversity of life, satisfies our deepest aspirations, and powerfully raises the soul above the things of time.

But the interest is heightened when we turn our thoughts to ourselves, and contemplate ourselves as members of this great spiritual community. The feeling of our dignity and our power is increased when we say, what each of us may say, "My existence is not in vain and aimless; I am a necessary link in the great chain of being which reaches from the awakening of the first man to perfect consciousness of his existence, onward through eternity; all the great and wise and noble that have ever appeared among men, those benefactors of the human race whose names I find recorded in the world's history, and the many others whose benefits have outlived their names, all have laboured for me; I have entered into their labours; I follow their footsteps on this earth where they dwelt, where they scattered blessings as they went along. I may, as soon as I will, assume the sublime task which they have resigned, of making our common brotherhood ever wiser and happier; I may continue to build where they had to cease their labours; I may bring nearer to its completion the glorious temple which they had to leave unfinished."

"But"—some one may say—"I too, like them, must rest from my labours." Oh! this is the sublimest thought of all! If I assume this noble task, I can never reach its end; and so surely as it is my vocation to assume it, I can never cease *to act*, and hence can never cease *to be*. That which men call Death cannot interrupt my activity; for my work must go on to its completion, and it cannot be completed in Time; hence my existence is not limited by Time, and I am Eternal: with the assumption of this great task, I have also laid hold of Eternity. I raise my head boldly to the threatening rock, the raging flood, or the fiery tempest, and say—"I am Eternal, and I defy your might! Break all upon me! and thou Earth, and thou Heaven, mingle in the wild tumult, and all ye elements, foam and fret yourselves, and crush in your conflict the last atom of the body which I call mine!—my WILL, secure in its own firm purpose, shall soar undisturbed and bold over the wreck of the universe: —for I have entered upon my vocation, and it is more enduring than ye are: it is ETERNAL, and I am ETERNAL like it."

LECTURE IV. The Vocation of the Scholar

I HAVE to-day to speak of the Vocation of the Scholar. I stand in a peculiar relation to this subject. All, or most of you, have chosen knowledge as the business of your lives; and I have made the same choice:—all of you, I presume, apply your whole energies, to fill honourably the station to which you aspire; and I too have done and do the like. I have to speak as a Scholar, before future Scholars, of the Scholar's vocation. I must examine the subject to its foundation; exhaust it, if I can; hold back nothing in my representation of the truth. And if I discover for the Scholar a vocation most honourable, most lofty, and distinguished above that of all other classes of men, how is it possible for me to lay it before you without exceeding the limits of modest expression, without seeming to undervalue other vocations, without being apparently blinded by self-conceit? But I speak as a philosopher, whose duty it is strictly to define all his ideas. I cannot exclude this idea from the system of which it is a necessary part. I dare not keep back any part of the truth which I recognise. It still remains true; and modesty itself is subordinate to it:—it is a false modesty which is violated by truth. Let us then consider our subject in the first place with indifference, as if it had no relation to ourselves: let us treat it as an idea belonging to a world quite foreign to our own. Let us on that account look with the greater strictness to our arguments. Let us never forget, what I hope I have already impressed upon you with some success, that every station in life is necessary; that each deserves our respect; that not the station itself, but the worthy fulfilment of its duties, does honour to a man; and that we only merit esteem the nearer we approach to the perfect performance of the duties assigned to us in the order of things; that therefore the Scholar has reason to be of all others the most modest, because an aim is set before him of which he must continually fall far short, because he has a most elevated ideal to reach, which commonly he approaches only at the greatest distance.

There are many tendencies and powers in man, and it is the vocation of each individual to cultivate *all* his powers, so far as he is able to do so. Among others is the social impulse; which offers him a new and peculiar form of cultivation, that for society, and affords an unusual facility for culture in general There is nothing prescribed to man on this subject; whether he shall cultivate all his faculties as a whole, unaided and by nature alone, or mediately through society. The first is difficult, and in no wise advances society; hence in the social state each individual rightfully selects his own part of the common culture, leaves the rest to his fellows, and expects that they will allow him to share the benefits of their culture, as he permits them to participate in the advantages of his own: and this is the origin and ground of the distinction of classes in society.

Such are the results arrived at in our previous discourses. For an arrangement of these different classes according to the ideas of Pure Reason, which is quite possible, a foundation must be sought in a complete enumeration of all the natural capacities and wants of man; not, however, of his merely artificial wants. A particular class in society may be devoted to the cultivation of each faculty, or, what is the same thing, to the satisfaction of each want founded on an original impulse in human nature. We reserve this inquiry for another occasion, that we may now enter upon one which lies nearer to us.

If a question should arise as to the perfection or imperfection of a state of society arranged on the principles which we have already propounded, (and every society does so arrange itself by the natural tendencies of man, without foreign guidance, as was shown in our inquiry into the origin of society), if, I say, such a question should arise, the answer to it would pre-suppose the solution of the following query: "Is the development and satisfaction of *all* the wants of man, and indeed the *harmonious* development and satisfaction of them all, provided for in the given state of society?" Is this provided for, then the society, as a society, is perfect; that is, not that it has attained its final purpose, which as we have previously shown is impossible; but that it is so arranged that it must of necessity continually approximate thereto: is this not provided for, then society may indeed by some happy chance be impelled forward in the way of culture; but that cannot be calculated on with certainty, for it may with as much probability be carried by some unlucky occurrence in the opposite direction.

A provision for the harmonious development of all the faculties of man pre-supposes an acquaintance with them all, a knowledge of all his tendencies and w r ants, a complete survey of his whole being. But this perfect knowledge of human nature is itself founded on a faculty which must be developed; for there is certainly an impulse in man *to know*, and particularly to know that which affects himself. The development of this faculty, however, demands all the time and energy of a man: if there be any want common to mankind which urgently requires that a particular class be set aside for its satisfaction, it is this.

The mere knowledge, however, of the faculties and wants of man, without an acquaintance with the means of developing and satisfying them, would be not only a most sorrowful and discouraging, but also a vain and perfectly useless, acquirement. He acts a most unfriendly part towards me, who points out to me my defects without at the same time showing me the means [of ?] supplying them; who raises me to the feeling of my wants without enabling me to satisfy them. Would that he had rather left me in brutish ignorance! In short, this would not be such knowledge as society requires, and for which a particular class of men is needed, to whom the possession of it may be committed; for this knowledge does not aim at the perfection of the species, and through that perfection at its harmonious combination, as it ought to do: hence to this knowledge of *wants* there must be added a *knowledge of the means by which they may be satisfied;* and this knowledge properly devolves upon the same class, because the one cannot be complete, and still less can it be active and living, without the other. Knowledge of the first kind is founded on the principles of Pure Reason, and is *philosophical;* that of the second, partly on Experience, and is in so far *philosophico-historical;* not merely historical, for I must connect the purposes which can only be recognised philosophically, with their appropriate objects revealed in Experience, in order to be able to recognise the latter as the means to the attainment of the former.

If, however, this knowledge is to become useful to society, it is not sufficient to ascertain what faculties belong essentially to man, and through what means they may be developed; such knowledge would still remain quite unproductive. It must proceed a step farther, in order to secure the wished-for benefits: we must also know on what particular grade of cultivation the society to which we belong stands at a particular point of time; to what particular stage it has next to ascend, and what are the means at its command for that purpose. Now on the grounds of Reason alone; on the supposition of Experience in the abstract, but prior to all actual Experience, we can calculate the direction which human progress must take; we can declare approximately the particular steps by which it must pass to the attainment of a definite stage of cultivation; but to declare the particular step on which it actually stands at a given point of time is impossible for Reason alone; for this, Experience must be questioned, the events of the past must be examined, but with an eye purified by philosophy; we must look around us, and consider our contemporaries. This last part of the knowledge needful to society is thus purely *historical.*

The three branches of knowledge which we have pointed out, when combined together—(and without such union they will be found of but little avail)—constitute what is called *learning*, or at least what alone ought to be so called; and he who devotes his life to the acquisition of this knowledge is a Scholar.

But every individual must not attempt to grasp the whole extent of human learning in all these three forms of knowledge; that would be impossible for most men; and therefore the striving after it would be fruitless, and the whole life of a member, who might have been of much value to society, would disappear without society reaping the slightest advantage from it. Each individual may mark out for himself a particular portion of this territory; but each ought to cultivate his part according to all the three views,—*philosophically, philosophico-historically*, and *historically*. And I now declare beforehand (what I shall further illustrate at another time) that you may in the meantime at least receive it on my testimony, that the study of a profound philosophy does not render the acquisition of empirical knowledge a superfluous labour, if that knowledge be well grounded; but that it rather proves the necessity of such knowledge in the most convincing manner. The common purpose of these different branches of knowledge has already been pointed out; viz. that by their means provision may be made for the uniform but constantly progressive development of all the faculties of man: and hence arises the true vocation of the Scholar; *the most widely extended survey of the actual advancement of the human race in general, and the steadfast promotion of that advancement*. I must impose some restraint upon myself, that I may not allow my feelings to expatiate upon the elevated idea which is now brought before you; the path of rigid inquiry is not yet ended. Yet I must remark, in passing, what it really is which they would do who should seek to check the free progress of knowledge. I say *would* do; for how can I know whether such persons really exist or not? Upon the progress of knowledge the whole progress of the human race is immediately dependent: he who retards that, hinders this also. And he who hinders this, what character does he assume towards his age and posterity? Louder than with a thousand voices, *by his actions* he proclaims into the deafened ear of the world present and to come "As long as I live at least, the men around me shall not become wiser or better; for in their progress I too, notwithstanding all my efforts to the contrary, should be dragged forward in some direction; and this I detest. I will not become more enlightened, I will not become nobler. Darkness and perversion are my elements, and I will summon all my powers together that I may not be dislodged from them."—Humanity may endure the loss of everything: all its possessions may be torn away without infringing its true dignity; all but the possibility of improvement. Coldly and craftily, as the enemy of mankind pictured to us in the Bible, these foes of man have calculated and devised their schemes, and explored the holiest depths to discover a point at which to assail humanity, so that they might crush it in the bud; and they have found it. Humanity turns indignantly from the picture.——We return to our investigation.

Knowledge is itself a branch of human culture; that branch must itself be further advanced if all the faculties of man are to be continuously developed; hence it is the duty of the Scholar, as of every man who has chosen a particular condition of life, to strive for the advancement of knowledge, and chiefly of his own peculiar department of knowledge; it is his duty as it is the duty of every man in his own department; yes, and it is much more his duty. It is for him to watch over and promote the advancement of other departments; and shall he himself not advance? Upon his progress, the progress of all other departments of human culture is dependent: he should always be in advance to open the way for others, to explore their future path, and to lead them forward upon it; and shall he remain behind? From that moment he would cease to be what he ought to be; and being nothing else, would then be nothing. I do not say that every Scholar must actually extend the domain of knowledge, that may not be within his power: but I do say that he *must strive* to extend it; that he must not rest, that he must not think his duty sufficiently performed, until he have extended it. So long as he lives he may yet accomplish this. Does death overtake him before he has attained his purpose? then he is released from his duties in this world of appearances, and his earnest endeavour will be accounted to him for the deed. If the following maxim be applicable to all men, it is more especially applicable to the Scholar: that he forget what he *has done* as soon as it is accomplished, and constantly direct his whole thoughts upon what he has yet *to do*. He has advanced but little way indeed, whose field of exertion does not extend its boundaries at every step he takes in it.

The Scholar is destined in a peculiar manner for society: his class, more than any other, exists only through society and for society: it is thus his peculiar duty to cultivate the social talents, an openness to receive, and a readiness to communicate knowledge, in the first place and in the highest degree. Receptivity must already be developed in him if he has thoroughly mastered the requisite empirical sciences. He must be thoroughly conversant with the labours of those who have gone before him in his own department, and this knowledge he cannot have acquired otherwise than by instruction, either oral or literary; he cannot have arrived at it by mere reflection on the principles of Reason. But he should at all times maintain this receptivity by means of new acquirements, and endeavour to preserve himself from a growing insensibility to foreign opinions and modes of thought, which is so common even among the most independent thinkers; for no one is so well informed but he may still continue to learn, and may have something very necessary yet to learn; and it is seldom that any one is so ignorant that he cannot teach something to the most learned, which the latter did not know before. Readiness of communication is always needed by the Scholar, for he possesses his knowledge not for himself, but for society. This he must practise from his youth, and keep in constant activity, through *what means*, we shall inquire at the proper time.

The knowledge which he has acquired for society he must now actually apply to the uses of society; he must rouse men to the feeling of their true wants, and make them acquainted with the means of satisfying these. Not that he should enter with them into the deep inquiries which he himself has been obliged to undertake, in order to find some certain and secure foundation of truth: that would be an attempt to make all men Scholars like himself, which is impossible, and of no advantage for the purposes of life; the other forms of human activity must also be prosecuted, and to that end there are other classes of men; if they devoted their time to learned inquiries, the Scholars themselves would soon cease to be Scholars. How then *can* he spread abroad his knowledge, and how *ought* he to do so? Society could not subsist without trust in the honesty and skill of others; this confidence is deeply impressed upon our hearts, and by a peculiar favour of Nature we never possess it in a higher degree than when we most need the honesty and skill of others. The Scholar may securely reckon upon this trust in his honesty and skill, as soon as he has earned it as he ought. Further, there is in all men a feeling of truth, which indeed is not sufficient in itself, but must be developed, proved, and purified; and to do this is the task of the Scholar. This feeling is not sufficient in itself to lead the unlearned to all the truth of which they stand in need; but when it has not become artificially falsified (which indeed is often the work of some who call themselves Scholars) it is always sufficient to enable them, even without deep argument, to recognise truth when another leads them to her presence. On this intuitive feeling of truth the Scholar too may rely. Thus, so far as we have yet unfolded the idea of his vocation, the Scholar is, by virtue of it, the *Teacher* of the human race.

But he has not only to make men *generally* acquainted with their wants, and with the means of satisfying these wants; he has likewise, *in particular*, at all times and in all places, to teach them the wants arising out of the special condition in which they stand, and to lead them to the appropriate means of reaching the peculiar objects which they are

30

there called upon to attain. He sees not merely the present, he sees also the future: he sees not merely the point which humanity now occupies, but also that to which it must next advance if it remain true to its final end, and do not wander or turn back from its legitimate path. He cannot desire to hurry forward humanity at once to the goal which perhaps gleams brightly before his own vision; the road cannot be overleaped; he must only take care that it do not stand still, and that it do not turn back. In this respect the Scholar is the *Guide* of the human race.

I remark here expressly, that in this as in all his other avocations, the Scholar is subject to the rule of the moral law, of the requisite harmony of his own being. He acts upon society; it is founded on the idea of freedom; it, and every member of it, is free; and he dares not approach it otherwise than by moral means. The Scholar will never be tempted to bring men to the adoption of his convictions by coercion or the use of physical force: in the present age it ought to be unnecessary to throw away a single word upon this folly: neither will he deceive them. Setting aside the fact that he would thereby offend against himself, and that the duties of the man are in every case higher than those of the Scholar: he would also thereby offend against society. Each individual in society ought to act from his own free choice, from his own mature and settled conviction; he ought to be able to look upon himself as a joint object of all his actions, and be regarded as such by all his fellow-men. He who is deceived, is used only as a means by which another may attain his purpose.

The ultimate purpose of each individual man, as well as of all society, and consequently of all the labours of the Scholar in society, is the moral elevation of all men. It is the duty of the Scholar to have this final object constantly in view, never to lose sight of it in all that he does in society. But no one can successfully labour for the moral improvement of his species who is not himself a good man. We do not teach by words alone, we also teach much more impressively by example; and every one who lives in society owes it a good example, because the power of example has its origin in the social relation. How much more is this due from the Scholar, who ought to be before all others in every branch of human culture? If he be behind in the first and highest of them all, that to which all the others tend, how can he be the pattern which he ought to be, and how can he suppose that others will follow his teachings, which he himself contradicts before all men in every action of his life? The words which the founder of the Christian Religion addressed to his disciples apply with peculiar force to the Scholar,—"Ye are the salt of the earth: if the salt have lost its savour, wherewith shall it be salted?"—if the chosen among men be depraved, where shall we seek for moral good? Thus, in this last respect, the Scholar ought to be *morally* the *best* man of his age; he ought to exhibit in himself the highest grade of moral culture then possible.

This is our common vocation,—this our common destiny. A happy vocation it is which calls upon you to do that, as your own peculiar occupation, which all men must do by reason of their common destiny as men; to employ all your time and powers upon that alone for which other men must hoard up time and power with wise parsimony; to have for your employment, your business, the sole everyday labour of your life, what only comes to others as sweet refreshment after toil! It is an invigorating, soul-elevating thought which each one among you, who is worthy of his calling, may entertain, "To me also, for my part, is entrusted the culture of my own and following ages; from my labours will proceed the course of future generations, the history of nations who are yet to be. To this am I called, to bear witness to the Truth: my life, my fortunes are of little moment; the results of my life are of infinite moment. I am a Priest of Truth; I am in her pay; I have bound myself to do all things, to venture all things, to suffer all things for her. If I should be persecuted and hated for her sake, if I should even meet death in her service, what wonderful thing is it I shall have done? what but that which I clearly ought to do?"

I know how much I have now said; I know too, that an effeminate and nerveless generation will tolerate neither these feelings nor the expression of them; that with a timorous voice which betrays its inward shame, it stigmatizes as extravagance everything which is above its reach; that it turns away its eyes with agony from a picture in which it beholds nothing but its own enervation and disgrace; that everything vigorous and elevating is to it as every touch to one diseased in all his limbs. I know all this; but I know too where I speak. I speak before young men who are at present secured by their youth against this utter enervation; and along with a manly morality, and by means of it, I would deeply impress such feelings on their souls as may preserve them for the future also from such effeminacy. I avow it freely, that from the point on which Providence has placed me, I too would willingly contribute something to extend in every direction, as far as my native tongue can reach and farther if possible, a more manly tone of thought, a stronger sense of elevation and dignity, a more ardent zeal to fulfil our destiny at every hazard; so that when you shall have left this place and are scattered abroad in all directions, I may one day know in you, wherever you may dwell, men whose chosen friend is Truth, who adhere to her in life and in death, who receive her when she is cast out by all the world, who take her openly under their protection when she is traduced and calumniated, who for her sake will joyfully bear the cunningly concealed enmity of the great, the dull sneer of the coxcomb, and the compassionating shrug of the fool. With this view I have now spoken; and in everything which I may address to you in future, I shall have the same ultimate design.

LECTURE V. Examination of Rousseau's Doctrines Concerning the Influence of Art and Science on the Well-Being of Man

THE combating of error is of no important advantage in the discovery of truth. If truth be once derived by just deduction from its essential principles, it follows without express refutation that everything opposed to it must necessarily be false; and if the whole path, which must be traversed in order to arrive at certain knowledge, lie clear before our view, we can at the same time easily observe the by-ways which lead from it towards erroneous opinions, and shall even be able readily to indicate to every wanderer the precise point from which he has gone astray. For every truth can be derived only from one fundamental principle. What the fundamental principle is, upon which each problem of human knowledge may be solved, it is the province of a fundamental philosophy to declare; how each principle should be followed out to its consequences, universal logic must teach; and thus the true as well as the false may be easily ascertained.

But the consideration of opposite opinions is of great value in imparting distinct and clear views of *discovered* truth. In comparing truth with error, we are obliged to note with greater accuracy the distinctive marks of both; and our conceptions of them acquire sharper precision and greater clearness. I now avail myself of this method to give you a short and plain view of what has been already brought forward in these lectures.

I have placed the vocation of man in the continual advancement of culture, and in the harmonious development of all his faculties and wants; and I have assigned to that class whose duty it is to watch over the progress and harmony of this development, a most honourable place in human society.

No man has opposed this truth more decidedly, on more plausible grounds, or with more powerful eloquence, than Rousseau. To him the advancement of culture is the sole cause of all human depravity. According to him there is no salvation for man but in a State of Nature; and—what indeed flows most accurately from his principles—that class of men who most effectually promote the advancement of culture, the Scholar-class, is at once the source and centre of all human misery and corruption.

Such a theory has been propounded by a man who has himself

cultivated his mental faculties in a very high degree. With all the power which he acquired by this superior cultivation, he laboured, wherever it was possible, to convince mankind of the justice of his doctrines, to persuade them to return to that State of Nature which he so much commended. To him retrogression was progress, and that forsaken State of Nature the ultimate end which a now marred and perverted humanity must finally attain. Thus he did precisely that which we do, he laboured to advance humanity according to his own ideas, and to aid its progress towards its highest end. He did that precisely which he himself so bitterly censured; his actions stand in opposition to his principles.

The same contradiction reigns in his principles themselves. What excited him to action but some impulse of his heart? Had he examined into this impulse, and connected it with that which led him into error, he would then have had unity and harmony both in his actions and in his conclusions. If we can reconcile the first contradiction, we shall, at the same time, have reconciled the second; the point of agreement of the first is likewise that of the second. We shall discover this point, we shall solve the contradiction, we shall understand Rousseau better than he understood himself, and we shall then discover him to be in perfect harmony with himself and with us.

Whence did Rousseau derive this extraordinary theory, maintained indeed partially by others before him, but as a whole so completely opposed to the general faith? Did he deduce it by reason from some higher principle? Oh no! Rousseau did not penetrate on any side to the confines of human knowledge; he does not appear ever to have proposed such an investigation to himself. What truth he possessed, he founded immediately on his feelings; and his knowledge has therefore the faults common to all knowledge founded on mere undeveloped feeling, that it is partly uncertain, because man cannot render to himself a complete account of his feelings; that the true is mixed up with the untrue, because a judgment resting upon feeling alone regards as of like meaning things which are yet essentially different. Feeling does not err; but the judgment errs, because it misinterprets feeling, and mistakes a compound for a pure feeling. From these undeveloped feelings, upon which Rousseau grounds his reflections, he proceeds with perfect justice: once in the region of syllogism, he is in harmony with himself, and hence carries the reader who can think with him, irresistibly along. Had he allowed his feelings to influence the *course* of his inquiries, they would have brought him back to the right path from which they had first led him astray. To have erred less than he did, Rousseau must have possessed either more or less acuteness of intellect

36

than he actually did possess; and so he who reads his works must, in order not to be led astray by them, possess either a much higher or a much lower degree of acuteness than he possessed; he must be either a complete thinker, or no thinker at all.

Separated from the great world, and guided by his pure feeling and lively imagination, Rousseau had sketched a picture of society, and particularly of the Scholar-class, with whose labours he especially occupied himself, *as they ought to be*, and as they necessarily must and would be, if they followed the guidance of common feeling. He came into the great world; he cast his eyes around him, and what were his sensations when the world and its Scholars, *as they actually were*, met his gaze! He saw, at its most fearful extreme, that scene which every one may see who turns his eyes towards it;[1]—men bowed down to the dust like beasts, chained to the earth regardless of their high dignity and the divinity within them; saw their joys, their sorrows, their whole existence, dependent on the satisfaction of a base sensuality whose demands rose higher with every gratification; saw them careless of right or wrong, holy or unholy, in the satisfaction of their appetites, and ever ready to sacrifice humanity itself to the desire of the moment; saw them ultimately lose all *sense* of right and wrong, and place wisdom in selfish cunning, and duty in the gratification of lust; saw them at last place their glory in this degradation and their honour in this shame, and even look down with contempt on those who were not *so* wise, and not *so* virtuous as themselves; saw those who ought to have been the teachers and guides of the nation sunk into the accommodating slaves of its corruption; those who ought to have given to the age a character of wisdom and of earnestness, assiduously catching the tones of the reigning folly and the predominant vice; heard them ask, for the guidance of their inquiries, not, Is it true? is it good and noble? but, Will it be well received? not, What will *humanity* gain by it? but, What shall *I* gain by it? how much gold, or what prince's favour, or what beauty's smile? saw them even look on this mode of thought as their highest honour, and bestow a compassionating shrug on the imbeciles who understood not like, them to propitiate the spirit of the time; saw talent, and art, and knowledge, united in the despicable task of extorting a more delicate enjoyment from nerves already wasted in pleasure, or in the detestable attempt to palliate or justify human depravity, to raise it to the rank of virtue, and wholly demolish everything which yet placed a barrier in its way; saw at length, and learned it by his own unhappy experience, that those unworthy men

---

[1]The reader will bear in mind that these Lectures were delivered in 1794, during the Revolutionary Epoch in France.

were sunk so low that the last misgiving which truth once produced within them, the last doubt which its presence called into being, having utterly disappeared, they became quite incapable of even examining its principles; that even with the demand for inquiry ringing in their ears, they could only answer, "Enough! it is not true, we do not wish it to be true, for it is no gain to us." He saw all this, and his strained and disappointed feelings revolted against it. With deep indignation he rebuked his Age.

Let us not blame him for this sensibility, it is the mark of a noble soul: he who feels the godlike within him, will often thus sigh upwards to eternal Providence: "These then are my brethren! these the companions whom thou hast given me on the path of earthly existence! Yes, they bear my shape, but our minds and hearts are not related; my words are to them a foreign speech, and theirs to me: I hear the sound of their voices, but there is nothing in my heart to give them a meaning! Oh eternal Providence! wherefore didst thou cause me to be born among such men? or if it were necessary that I should be born among them, wherefore didst thou give me these feelings, this longing presentiment of something better and higher? why didst thou not make me like them? why didst thou not make me base even as they are? I could then have lived contentedly among them." Ye do well to reprove his melancholy, and censure his discontent, ye to whom all around you seems good; ye do well to commend to him the contentment with which ye derive enjoyment from all things, and the modesty with which ye accept men as they are! He would have been as modest as ye are, had he been tormented with as few noble aspirations. Ye cannot rise to the conception of a better state, and for you truly the present is well enough.

In this fulness of bitter feeling, Rousseau was now incapable of seeing anything but the object which had called it forth. Sensualism reigned triumphant; that was the source of the evil: he would know how to destroy this empire of sensualism at all hazards, cost what it might. No wonder that he fell into the opposite extreme. Sensualism shall not reign; it cannot reign when it is destroyed, when it ceases to exist; *or* when it is not developed, when it has not acquired power. Hence Rousseau's State of Nature.

In the State of Nature the faculties peculiar to man shall not be cultivated; they shall not even be distinguished. Man shall have no other wants than those of his animal nature; he shall live like the beast on the meadow beside him. It is true that in this State none of those crimes against which Rousseau's feelings so strongly revolted would find a place; man would eat when he hungered, and drink when he was athirst, whatever he found before him; and, when satisfied, would have no interest in depriving others of that which he could not use himself. Once satiated himself, any one might eat or drink before him what and how much soever he would, for now he desires rest, and has no time to disturb others. In the anticipation of the future lies the true character of humanity; it is therefore the source of all human vice. Shut out the source, and vice is no more; and Rousseau did effectually exclude it from his State of Nature.

But it is also true that man, as surely as he is man and not a beast, is not destined to remain in this condition. Vice, indeed, would thus cease; but with it Virtue, and Reason too, would be destroyed. Man becomes an irrational creature; there is a new race of animals; men no longer exist.

There can be no doubt that Rousseau acted honourably with men: he longed himself to live in that State of Nature which he so warmly recommended to others, and showed throughout every indication of this desire. We may then put the question to him, what was it in truth which he sought in this State of Nature? He felt himself imprisoned, crushed down by manifold wants, and—what is indeed no great evil to the majority of men, but the bitterest oppression to such a man as he was,—he was often seduced from the path of rectitude and virtue by these wants. Living in a State of Nature, he thought he should be without these wants; and be spared so much pain from their denial, and so much yet bitterer pain from their dishonourable gratification; he should then be *at peace with himself.* He also found himself oppressed on every side by others, because he stood in the way of the satisfaction of their desires. Man does not do evil in vain and for no purpose, thought Rousseau, and we with him; none of those who injured him would have done so, had they not felt these desires. Had all around him lived in a State of Nature, he should then have been *at peace with others.* Thus Rousseau desired undisturbed tranquillity within and without. Well: but we inquire further—To what purpose would he apply this unruffled peace? Undoubtedly to that to which he applied the measure of rest that did actually belong to him; to reflection on his destiny and his duties, thereby to ennoble himself and his fellow-men. But how was that possible in the state of animalism which he assumed, how was it possible without the previous culture which he could only obtain in the state of civilization? He thus insensibly transplanted himself and society into this State of Nature, *with all that cultivation which they could only acquire by coming out of the State of Nature;* he imperceptibly assumed that they had already left it and had traversed the whole path of civilization, and yet had not left it and had not become civilized. And thus we have arrived at Rousseau's false assumption, and are now able to solve his paradoxes without any serious difficulty.

Rousseau would not transplant men back into a State of Nature with respect to spiritual culture, but only with respect to independence of the desires of sense. And it is certainly true, that as man approaches nearer to the highest end of his existence, it must constantly become easier for him to satisfy his sensual wants; that his physical existence must cost him less labour and care; that the fruitfulness of the soil must increase, the climate become milder; an innumerable multitude of new discoveries and inventions be made to diversify and facilitate the means of subsistence; that further, as Reason extends her dominion, the wants of man will constantly diminish in strength, not as in a rude State of Nature in which he is ignorant of the delights of life, but because he can bear their deprivation; he will be ever equally ready to enjoy the best with relish, when it can be enjoyed without violation of duty, and to endure the want of everything which he cannot obtain with honour. Is this state considered ideal? in which respect it is unattainable like every other Ideal State, then it is identical with the golden age of sensual enjoyment without physical labour which the old poets describe. Thus what Rousseau, under the name of the State of Nature, and these poets under the title of the Golden Age, place *behind us*, lies actually *before us*. (It may be remarked in passing, that it is a phenomenon of frequent occurrence, particularly in past ages, that what we *shall become* is pictured as something which we already *have been;* and that what we have to attain is represented as something which we have formerly lost: a phenomenon which has its proper foundation in human nature, and which I shall explain on a suitable occasion.)

Rousseau forgot that humanity can and ought to approach nearer to this state only by care, toil, and struggle. Nature *is* rude and savage without the hand of man: and it *should be* so, that thereby man may be forced to leave his natural state of inactivity, and elaborate her stores; that thereby he himself, instead of a mere product of Nature, may become a free reasonable being. He does most certainly leave it; he plucks at all hazards the apple of knowledge, for the impulse is indestructibly implanted within him, to be like God. The first step from this state leads him to misery and toil: his wants are awakened, and clamorously demand gratification. But man is naturally indolent and sluggish, like matter from whence he proceeded. Hence arises the hard struggle between want and indolence: the first triumphs, but the latter bitterly complains. Now in the sweat of his brow he tills the field, and it frets him that it should bear thorns and thistles which he must uproot. Want is not the source of vice, it is the motive to activity and virtue; indolence, sluggishness, is the source of all vice. *How to enjoy as much as possible, how to do as little as possible?*—this is the question of a perverted nature, and the various attempts made to answer this question are its crimes. There is no salvation for man until this natural sluggishness is successfully combated, until he find all his pleasures and enjoyments in activity, and in activity alone. To that end pain is associated with the feeling of want. It should rouse us to activity.

This is the object of all pain; it is peculiarly the object of that pain which we experience at every view of the imperfection, depravity, and misery of our fellow men. He who does not feel this pain, this bitter indignation, is a mean-souled man. He who does feel it, ought to endeavour to release himself from it, by directing all his powers to the task of improving, as far as possible, all within his sphere and around him. And even supposing that his labours should prove fruitless, and he should see no use in their continuance, still the feeling of his own activity, the consciousness of his own power which he calls forth to the struggle against the general depravity, will cause him to forget this pain. Here Rousseau failed. He had energy, but energy rather of suffering than of action; he felt strongly the miseries of mankind, but he was far less conscious of his own power to remedy them; and thus as he felt himself he judged of others; as he conducted himself amid his own peculiar sorrows, so did humanity at large, in his view, endure the common lot. He took account of its sorrows; but he forgot the power which the human race possesses,—*to help itself.*

Peace be with his ashes, and blessings upon his memory! He has done his work. He has kindled fire in many souls, who have carried on what he began. But he wrought almost without being conscious of his own influence; he wrought without intending to rouse others to the work, without weighing their labour against the sum of general evil and depravity. This want of endeavour after self-activity reigns throughout his whole system of ideas. He is the man of passive sensibility, not at the same time of proper active resistance to its power. His lovers, led astray by passion, become virtuous; but we do not rightly perceive how they become so. The struggle of reason against passion,—the victory, gradual and slow, gained only by exertion, labour, and pain,—that most interesting and instructive of all spectacles, he conceals from our view. His pupil is developed by himself alone. The teacher does little more than remove the obstructions to his growth, and leave the rest to the care of Nature. She must henceforth and for ever retain him under her guardianship. The energy, ardour, and firm determination to war against and to subdue her, he has not taught him. Among good men he will be happy; but among bad,—and where is it that the majority are not bad?—he will suffer unspeakable misery. Thus Rousseau throughout depicted Reason *at peace*, but not *in strife;—he weakened Sense, instead of strengthening Reason.*

I have undertaken the present inquiry in order to solve the famous paradox which stood so directly opposed to our principles: but not for that purpose alone. I would at the same time show you, by the example of one of the greatest men of our own age, *what you ought not to be*. I would, by his example, unfold to you an important lesson for your whole life. You are now learning, by philosophic inquiry, what the men *ought to be* with whom you have not as yet generally entered into any near, close, and indissoluble relations. You will soon come into closer relations with them. You will find them very different in reality from what your philosophy would have them to be. The nobler and better you are yourselves, the more painfully will you feel the experience which awaits you. Be not overcome by this pain, but overcome it by action: it does not exist without a purpose; it is a part of the plan of human improvement. To stand aloof and lament over the corruption of man, without stretching forth a hand to diminish it, is weak effeminacy; to cast reproach and bitter scorn on man, without showing him how he can become better, is unfriendly. Act! act!—it is to that end we are here. Should we fret ourselves that others are not *so perfect* as we are, when we ourselves are only *somewhat less imperfect* than they? Is not this our greatest perfection,—the vocation which has been given to us, —that we must labour for the perfecting of others? Let us rejoice in the prospect of that widely extended field which we are called to cultivate! Let us rejoice that power is given to us, and that our task is infinite!

Made in the USA
Las Vegas, NV
07 February 2024

85459075R00030